NAJC

FAMILIES
Like Mine

Marie-Therese Miller

Special thanks to Stephanie Garrity, Executive Director of Rainbows for All Children

Lerner Publications ◆ Minneapolis

For my family: John Edward, Michelle, Sean, Meghan, John Vincent, Erin, Elizabeth, and Greyson

Lerner Publications Company
An imprint of Lerner Publishing Group, Inc.
241 First Avenue North
Minneapolis, MN 55401 USA

For reading levels and more information, look up this title at www.lernerbooks.com.

Main body text set in Mikado a.
Typeface provided by HVD Fonts.

Designer: Emily Harris
Lerner team: Sue Marquis

Library of Congress Cataloging-in-Publication Data

Names: Miller, Maria-Therese, 1960- author.
Title: Families like mine / Maria-Therese Miller.
Description: Minneapolis : Lerner Publications, 2020. | Series: Many ways | Includes bibliographical references and index. | Audience: Ages 5–9 | Audience: Grades K-1 | Summary: "Families include one child and one parent, multiple parents and grandparents with many children, and everything in between. Explore diverse families and the many ways that they care for one another"— Provided by publisher.
Identifiers: LCCN 2019049904 (print) | LCCN 2019049905 (ebook) | ISBN 9781541598034 (library binding) | ISBN 9781728413686 (paperback) | ISBN 9781728400136 (ebook)
Subjects: LCSH: Families—Juvenile literature. | Interpersonal relations—Juvenile literature.
Classification: LCC HQ744 .M535 2020 (print) | LCC HQ744 (ebook) | DDC 306.85—dc23

LC record available at https://lccn.loc.gov/2019049904
LC ebook record available at https://lccn.loc.gov/2019049905

Manufactured in the United States of America
1-47994-48672-1/30/2020

OurFamilyWizard is proud to offer the Many Ways series. Since 2001, OurFamilyWizard has been dedicated to supporting communication between parents who are raising kids from separate homes. Over the years, the understanding of what a family looks like has changed. But no matter a family's shape or size, the meaning of family has always remained rooted in love and respect. We hope these books help children learn the many different ways to be.

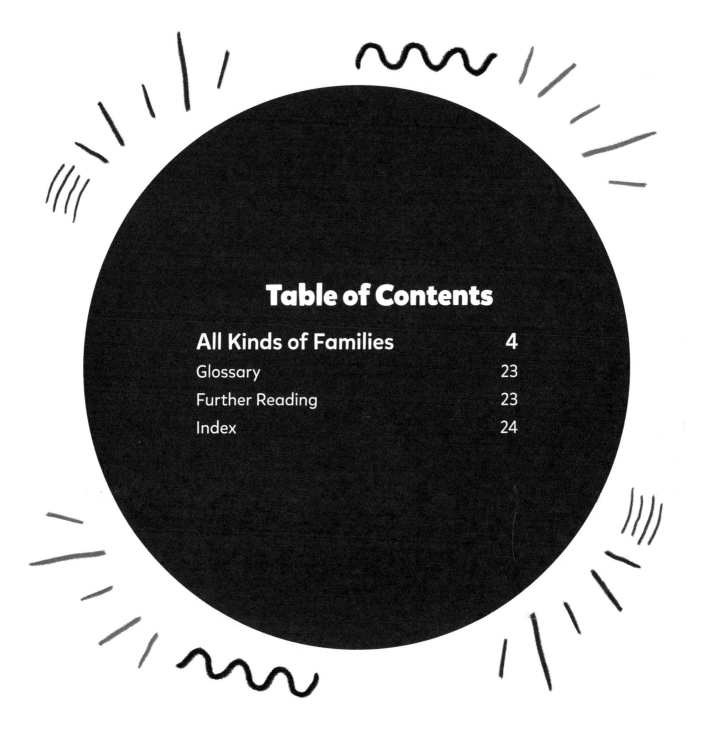

Table of Contents

All Kinds of Families

Families love and care for one another. Families can be big or small. Family members might live together or apart.

What kind of **FAMILY** do you have?

Some families have many **CHILDREN**. These families can be noisy.

Other families have one **CHILD**. They might be quiet.

Some children are **BORN** into families.

Other kids are **ADOPTED** or **FOSTERED** by families.

Families may have a mom and a dad. They might have one mom or one dad.

Some families have two moms or two dads.

Blended families have **STEPPARENTS**.

They can have **STEPSIBLINGS** too.

Sometimes, parents cannot take care of their children.

Then the other parent, **GRANDPARENTS**, or others might help.

A family may have many **RELATIVES** living together.

Grandparents, aunts, uncles, and cousins might share the same house.

Some families have two **HOMES** because the parents divorced or separated.

Children in these families might spend time at each parent's home.

PETS such as hamsters and dogs can be family members.

Animals need **LOVE** and **CARE** just as people do.

FAMILIES come in many shapes and sizes. They all talk and dream together. Families laugh and have fun.

Glossary

adopt: to make a child part of your family forever

blended family: a family that includes children of a previous marriage of one parent or both

divorce: to end a marriage

foster: to parent a child without adopting the child

grandparent: a parent of your mother or father

relative: a family member

stepparent: a mom or dad who married into a family

stepsibling: a stepparent's son or daughter by a former partner

Further Reading

Bullard, Lisa. *My Family, Your Family*. Minneapolis: Lerner Publications, 2015.

Families—There Are Many Kinds
http://www.cyh.com/HealthTopics/HealthTopicDetailsKids.aspx?p=335&np=282&id=1524

Family Tree Kids
https://www.familytreemagazine.com/kids/familytreekids/#

Military Kids Connect
https://militarykidsconnect.dcoe.mil/

Noemi, Fernández Selva. *All Ways Family*. Washington, DC: Magination, 2020.

Pettiford, Rebecca. *Different Families*. Minneapolis: Jump!, 2018.

Index

Photo Acknowledgments

Image credits: kali9/E+/Getty Images, pp. 4, 16; Maskot/Getty Images, p. 5; yellowsarah/iStock/Getty Images, p. 6; Blend Images - Inti St Clair/Getty Images, p. 7; Utah-based Photographer Ryan Houston/Moment/Getty Images, p. 8; DNF Style/Shutterstock.com, p. 9; images by Tang Ming Tung/Moment/Getty Images, p. 10; Hero Images/Getty Images, p. 11; vorDa/E+/Getty Images, p. 12; Inti St Clair/Getty Images, p. 13; Elizabethsalleebauer/RooM/Getty Images, p. 14; Terry Vine/DigitalVision/Getty Images, p. 15; Ariel Skelley/DigitalVision/Getty Images, p. 17; Ronnie Kaufman/DigitalVision/Getty Images, p. 18; PeopleImages/E+/Getty Images, p. 19; Wavebreakmedia/iStock/Getty Images, p. 20; Radius Images/Getty Images, p. 21; kali9/iStock/Getty Images, p. 22.

Cover: FatCamera/E+/Getty Images (top left); monkeybusinessimages/iStock/Getty Images (top right); kate_sept2004/E+/Getty Images (bottom left); paulaphoto/iStock/Getty Images (bottom right).